LEARNING ABOUT SEX

for the **Christian** family

Where Do Babies Come From?

For **Girls** ages **7-9** and **Parents**

CONCORDIA PUBLISHING HOUSE · SAINT LOUIS

Book 2 of the Learning about Sex Series

The titles in the series:

Book 1: Why Boys and Girls Are Different

Book 2: Where Do Babies Come From?

Book 3: How You Are Changing

Book 4: Sex and the New You

Book 5: Love, Sex, and God

Book 6: How to Talk Confidently with Your Child about Sex

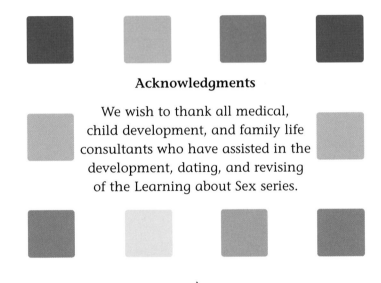

Acknowledgments

We wish to thank all medical,
child development, and family life
consultants who have assisted in the
development, dating, and revising
of the Learning about Sex series.

Copyright © 1982, 1988, 1995, 1998, 2008 Concordia Publishing House
3558 S. Jefferson Ave., St. Louis, MO 63118-3968
1-800-325-3040 • www.cph.org

All rights reserved. No part of this publication may be reproduced, stored in a retrieval system,
or transmitted, in any form or by any means, electronic, mechanical, photocopying, recording,
or otherwise, without the prior written permission of Concordia Publishing House.

From text originally written by Ruth Hummel

Illustrations by Janet McDonnell

Scripture quotations are from The Holy Bible, English Standard Version®.
Copyright © 2001 by Crossway Bibles, a publishing ministry of Good News Publishers, Wheaton, Illinois.
Used by permission. All rights reserved.

This publication may be available in braille, in large print, or on cassette tape for the visually impaired.
Please allow 8 to 12 weeks for delivery. Write to Lutheran Blind Mission, 7550 Watson Rd.,
St. Louis, MO 63119-4409; call toll-free 1-888-215-2455; or visit the Web site: www.blindmission.org.

Manufactured in China

1 2 3 4 5 6 7 8 9 10   17 16 15 14 13 12 11 10 09 08

Editor's Foreword

This book is one of a series of six designed to help parents communicate biblical values to their children in the area of sexuality. *Where Do Babies Come From?* is the second book in the series. It is written especially for girls ages 7 to 9 and, of course, for the parents, teachers, and other concerned grown-ups who will read the book to the child. (See the "Note to Grown-ups" on the next page for suggestions on using the book and ways to communicate Christian values in sex education in the home.)

Like its predecessor, the new Learning about Sex series provides information about the social-psychological and physiological aspects of human sexuality. Moreover, it does so from a distinctively Christian point of view, in the context of our relationship to the God who created us and redeemed us in Jesus Christ. The series presents sex as another good gift from God that is to be used responsibly.

Each book in the series is graded—in vocabulary and in the amount of information it provides. It answers the questions that persons at each age level typically ask.

Because children vary widely in their growth rates and interest levels, parents and other concerned adults will want to preview each book in the series, directing your child to the next graded book when she is ready for it.

In addition to reading each book, you can use them as starting points for casual conversation and when answering other questions a child might have.

This book can also be used as a mini-unit or as part of another course of study in a Christian school setting. Whenever the book is used in a classroom setting, it is important to let the parents know beforehand, since they have the primary responsibility for the sex education of their children. If used in a classroom setting, the books are designed for separate single-gender groups, the setting most conducive to open conversations about questions and concerns.

While parents will appreciate the help of the school, they will want to know what is being taught. As the Christian home and the Christian school work together, Christian values in sex education can be more effectively strengthened.

The Editors

A Note to Grown-ups

In story form, this book answers questions about sexuality that seven- to nine-year-olds typically ask—or wonder about. Many children this age will have difficulty reading the book on their own. So *do* plan to enjoy reading it *with* your child. Depending on her interest, read all of it at one time, or read one chapter at a time.

Make it just another book that you enjoy reading to or with your child at the usual times when you read together. Once you've read it, of course, you may want to read it again—next month or even next year, when your child is at a different developmental level and able to absorb more of the content.

Take your time as you read, expanding on the text when your child asks for further information. Most of all, use the occasion to wonder at the beauty and design of God's good gift of sexuality. After all, what we're most interested in is building in your child a reverent, wholesome, responsible attitude about human conception and birth. We want to communicate not only truthful and accurate information about sexuality, but especially a deep appreciation of God's marvelous design and purpose, and a sense of respect and responsibility toward all God has given. "God made me a girl—and His creation is wonderful!"

Here are five easy-to-remember guidelines (each beginning with a C) to keep in mind as you answer questions:

1. *Commend* your child for coming to you and for asking, especially if the question makes you uneasy! You want to keep the channels of communication open.

2. *Clarify* the question: "When you ask, 'Where do babies come from?' do you mean, 'How do they grow?' "

3. *Communicate* with simple, direct answers.

4. *Connect* your answer to what your child already knows (or thinks she knows): "Remember what you learned about . . . ? That will help you understand that . . ." Also, you may want to connect your child's question to other aspects of growing up, thereby avoiding the danger of isolating sex from the wider background of life in general.

5. *Care* must be taken to warn your child about the possibilities of abuse. You might want to work this into a discussion of appropriate behavior. "Your body belongs to you—including those private parts that your swimming suit covers. You don't show those parts or touch them in public. And other people should not touch your private parts either. No one has a right to do that unless it's a nurse or a doctor helping you to be well or someone who cares for you helping you to be clean. If anyone does touch your private parts, be sure to tell me. I want to keep you safe."

6. *Christ* Himself is with us and is guiding us in what we say and what we model about relationships. Share with your child: "Isn't it *wonderful* that Jesus, God's own Son, was born as a baby? He grew up—just as we do. So He knows what it's like when we feel lonely or afraid. He always did what was right—and He died on a cross—to pay for our sins. Now we can be sure that God, our Father, forgives us. And we can be glad that Jesus is there to help us grow as God's loving children."

Alisa Has a Birthday

Alisa was seven years old today. She could hardly wait to get home from school.

Her dad, her mom, and her grandma were all waiting. Grandma always came over when there was a birthday or something else special.

"You need me to help you celebrate, don't you?" she said with a wink. Alisa agreed as she gave her a hug. Then she saw her birthday cake.

"O-o-oh, it's cool!" she said. And it was! It had seven candles. With the family gathered around, she opened her presents. There was a set of dressed-up dolls, a pair of skates, the game she had wished for, and tickets to go to the park today.

"How did everyone know just what I wanted?" Alisa wondered. "They must know me pretty well."

After Alisa blew out the candles, her dad picked her up and gave her a big hug. Alisa giggled when she got her breath.

"Look how big our girl is getting, Mother," Dad said. "Do you still remember how she looked seven years ago today?"

"Seven years ago, Alisa, you had just been born," Mother said. "You looked beautiful to me! Maybe you were just another red and wrinkled baby to some people! But to me, you were perfect! I wondered how your fingers and toes could be so tiny. I saw that you had your dad's brown eyes. And I prayed, 'Thank You, God, for such a fine baby.' "

"Yep," said Dad. "We thought you were really something special. Crying loudly, but very special! We were so glad God gave you to us. And wow! Did you change our family!"

"I changed our family?" Alisa was surprised. "How could I do that? I was just a baby."

"Just a baby?" Dad laughed. "Before you came, Alisa, there were just Mother and I to love each other. But after you came, we had another person to love. Soon you learned to love us too. So then there was a lot more love in our family than ever before."

"You mean each new baby brings more love to a family?" Alisa asked. When Mother nodded, Alisa said, "Then every baby does change a family."

"That's right," Mother said. "Families are always changing. They change in different ways. A family grows larger whenever a baby is born or a child is adopted. And people in the family are always growing older, and the babies are always growing bigger."

"I know a family where the children are teenagers," Dad said. "They've grown taller than their mother and father."

"They'll be grown up soon," Alisa said. "When they move away, that will make their family smaller again."

"That's what happened to our family," Grandma said. "Our children got married. Then Grandpa and I were a small family again."

"Sometimes a family may have just a father or a mother. Or a family can grow larger when grandparents come to live with them," Mother said.

"Why don't you come and live here with us, Grandma?" Alisa asked. "Then our family would grow again."

"Someday," Grandma said, "maybe I will make this family grow bigger. Just like you did, Alisa, when you were born. When I first saw you, I knew for sure you belonged in this family. That straight, firm nose is your mother's, for sure."

"But how did I get her nose, Grandma?"

"Well, babies born into a family often look like someone else in their family. Of course, God doesn't make exact copies when He makes a new person. He makes each of us special—like no one else in the world."

"But what about John, next door?" Alisa said. "I wonder why he doesn't look like anyone in his family."

"That's because he was adopted into his family," Dad explained. "He was born to another mother. She loved him but could not take care of him. John's parents wanted someone just like him for their family, so they adopted him."

"What does that mean—*adopted* him?" Alisa asked.

"Well, Alisa, it means they decided to make him their own child. They love him as much as if he were born to them."

"That's another kind of family!" Alisa said.

"Families are different in many ways," said Mother. "Some families have just a mother or a father. Some families have only one child. Some families have many children. But in some important ways we are all the same. We are all people

✝ loved by God,

✝ living together,

✝ loving each other,

✝ celebrating good times together,

✝ helping each other through bad times, and

✝ caring about what happens to each other."

"It was God who thought of putting us into families," Dad said. "Wasn't it a good idea?"

"I'm glad God put me into this family," Alisa said. "It's just right for me."

"O families of the peoples, ascribe to the Lord glory and strength!" (Psalm 96:7)

A Trip to the Museum

"Well, I think I'm ready," said Mother. "Shall we go now?"

Alisa was so excited! She was going to the museum with Mother and Dad. It was a special treat. They had promised Alisa that she could take her friend Nate along too.

In the car, her Dad asked, "Well, Alisa, what are we going to see first?"

"Oh, the baby chicks are hatching!" Alisa didn't have any trouble deciding. "They are my favorite thing in the whole museum." And she told them all about the little, fuzzy yellow chickens sitting under the light to keep warm.

At last they were going up the steps of the museum. "Look, Mom, a balloon man! May I have a blue one? Please?"

"Okay," said Mother as she paid for the balloon. "But when will I ever get to see those chickens?"

"Come on, they're right over here," said Nate.

"Look at this," Alisa whispered. One little chick was just pecking through his eggshell. Alisa was so excited she almost stopped breathing. Peck! Peck! They could all hear the tiny sounds from inside the egg. They watched quietly until the eggshell fell apart.

"Ooh, how wet and tired he looks!" Nate said. "Now he'll have to sit and rest until his feathers start to dry and get fluffy."

"I know babies don't hatch like chicks do," Alisa said softly. "But I wonder just how they do get born."

"H-m-m-m," Dad said. "That's a big question."

"If you are finished watching the chickens," Mother said, "we may be able to find out over there by that sign."

"Oh, look! How tiny that baby is!" said Nate. "I have never seen a baby that little."

"Hardly anyone does! When a baby is that tiny," Mother explained, "he can't eat or even breathe for himself. He has to live inside his mother's body. God made a special place for a baby to grow. It is called a *uterus*."

"A *you-ter-us*?" The word sounded strange, but it wasn't hard to say.

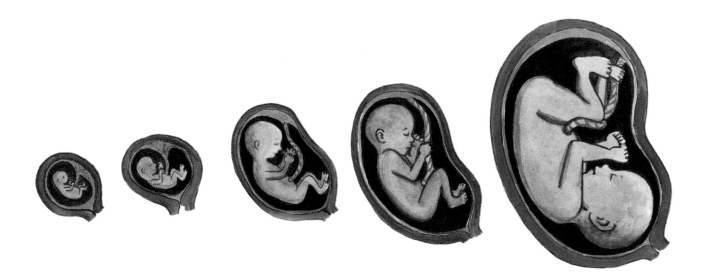

Nate asked, "What is the uterus like? Is it like a little box?"

"More like a little balloon," Mother said. "Look, I'll show you." She took Alisa's balloon, let some air out until it was about the size of a pear, and said, "It's just about this size. And it's hollow inside too."

"The tiny baby settles down near the side. The side of the uterus is much thicker than this balloon. That is where the baby grows."

"Here's a baby when it is bigger. Look!" Nate said. "See those little fingers and those tiny little toes! And look at that little mouth."

Alisa wondered aloud, "Can a baby eat with such a little mouth?"

"No, it can't eat when it is so tiny," Mother explained. "It does not need to eat while it is in the mother's uterus."

"The baby gets its food from the mother's body. See that cord going from the baby's tummy to the side of the uterus? Food from the mother's body comes to the baby's body through that cord so the baby can keep growing. The baby can't breathe yet either. So oxygen comes through that tube too."

"Was I ever so little that I couldn't breathe?" Alisa wondered.

"You sure were!" Dad said. "Even somebody as big as me was that small once."

"It was a good thing you both had a mother to be connected to," said Mother. "Do you know where your cord joined your body, Alisa?"

"Right in the middle some-where, I guess," Alisa answered with a little giggle. "At my belly button?"

"That's right!" Dad chuckled. "Sounds like you were buttoned onto your mother. The real name for that place is *navel.*"

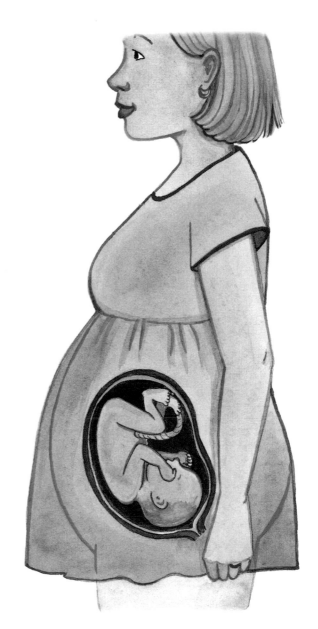

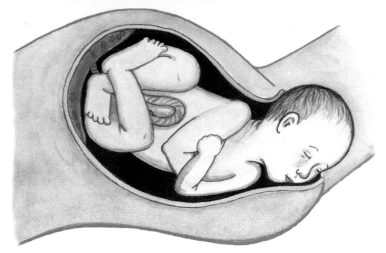

Another thing seemed strange to Alisa. "I wonder why these babies don't have any clothes on," she said.

"They don't need clothes," Mother said. "It's so warm and comfortable in the uterus."

"But how can they ever go to the bathroom?" Alisa asked.

"Oh, they don't have to." Mother pointed to the cord again. "That cord takes care of everything. While the food goes to the baby's body, the waste goes from the baby's body to the mother's."

"Oh, I see," Alisa said. "But it must get pretty crowded in there when the baby gets bigger."

Dad laughed. "It is cozy, all right. The baby has to lie all curled up, with his legs bent and tucked under his chin."

"Look how big this next baby is!" Alisa said. "Is there still enough room for such a big baby?"

"Bring me your balloon a minute," Dad said. "What would happen to this balloon if you blew more air into it?"

"I guess it would get bigger," Alisa said.

"That's the answer," said Dad.

"You mean the uterus gets bigger like a balloon?"

"That's right, Alisa," Mother said. "As the baby grows, there's always room for it. When the baby grows this big, the mother's body becomes big and round. Now everyone can see that the mother has a baby growing in her."

"You mean she gets chubby like Grandma calls herself?"

"No, no," Mother said. "It's not the same as being chubby."

"We say she is *pregnant*. After the baby is born, the uterus will slowly go back to its normal size again, just like when air goes out of a balloon!"

"How does the baby get born then? Does the uterus break open like when a balloon gets popped?"

"Oh, no, Alisa," Mother said. "The uterus has an opening something like a balloon has. That opening can stretch, too. When it is time for the baby to be born, it comes out through the opening."

"Is that how I was born?" Alisa asked.

"Yes, Alisa," Mother said. "That's how you and I and everyone in the whole world was born. That is God's way of bringing new people into the world."

"I don't understand it, but if it's God's plan, I think it must be wonderful. Don't you think so, Dad?"

Dad agreed. "That's why they call it 'the miracle of birth.' "

"I praise You, for I am fearfully and wonderfully made."
(Psalm 139:14)

Boys and Girls—Fathers and Mothers

"Hey, Alisa!" Someone was calling. Alisa looked outside. Nate and his little brother, Kip, were running through the rain to her porch.

"Can we play at your house?" they wanted to know.

"Sure," Alisa said. "Come on in. What do you want to play?"

"Well, we can't play ball, because it's raining," Nate said. "Besides, I have to take care of Kip. You know what four-year-old kids are like!"

"What can we play?" asked Alisa.

"I want to play house," said Kip. "Can I be the mother? I want to cook." He picked up a bowl from the kitchen counter and pretended to stir it with a big spoon.

Nate and Alisa laughed. "You can't be the mother, Kip," Alisa said. "You're a boy! Boys and girls can be cooks. But only girls can be mothers."

Kip wasn't sure about this. "But I can be anything I want when I get big," he insisted. "Dad said I could!"

"Dad meant you could be an airplane pilot, or a firefighter, or even a cook," Nate explained. "He didn't mean you could be a mother. Only girls can be mothers."

"That's right," Alisa chimed in. "God made girls with a special place where a baby can grow inside them." Alisa patted her tummy.

"I wonder why it's in their stomach." Kip looked puzzled. "With all the hot dogs and pancakes and ice cream?"

"It's not in the woman's stomach. It's in a special place called the uterus," Nate explained. "It's inside the body, so you can't see it."

"If you can't see it," Kip said, "how do you know I don't have one, too?"

"No way, Kip," said Alisa. "You can be sure you don't, because you are a boy. Boys have their own special body. They grow up to be fathers."

"You mean boys have to be fathers?" Kip sounded confused. "Can't I be a cowboy when I am big?"

"Of course, Kip," Nate laughed. "You can be a father as well as a cowboy or almost anything else you want to be."

"Oh, I'm so lucky," Kip sang. "Boys can be more things than girls."

"That's not what I said, Kip." Nate was tired of explaining everything.

"Girls can be many things too," said Alisa. "I can be a mother and a lot of other things. I can be a teacher, a firefighter, or even a doctor. Boys and girls are different, but one is not better than the other."

"We can learn about this from God. He loves us all the same, boys and girls, men and women," said Nate. "From Jesus we learn to treat all people with loving-kindness and respect, whoever they are."

"Well, okay. Then I'll be the father," Kip decided. "But I still want to be the cook too. I'm going to make some hamburgers." Kip started moving his arm, pretending he was flipping hamburgers.

"Male and female [God] created them, and He blessed them." (Genesis 5:2)

In Mother's Workroom

"Mother, where are you?" Alisa called when she got in the house. She was hungry.

"I'm here in the workroom," Mother answered. "Why don't you get a cookie and come and talk with me a while?"

I wonder how she knew I wanted a cookie? Alisa thought. Then she called, "May I have two, please?"

"Okay, Alisa," Mother answered. "But put the lid back on the cookie jar."

"M-m-m! These are good," Alisa said when she got to the workroom. "Thanks a lot."

"You sure had fun with Kip and Nate yesterday," Mother said as she arranged some silk flowers in three bunches.

"Uh-huh," Alisa said and took another bite. "I like playing with Nate and Kip. But Kip sure says some funny things."

"Like what?" Mother asked as she got out her glue gun and began to attach the flowers to a wreath.

"Well," Alisa said with her mouth still full of cookie, "Kip wondered why he couldn't be a mother. And he complained that babies are always messy and crying."

"Well, they do cry a lot. But that is the only way they can tell someone they're hungry or hurt or cold," Mother said gently, as she added some berries to the wreath.

"You mean crying is like their way of talking?" Alisa was surprised at that.

Mother nodded. "If they could say, 'Mommy, I want my diaper changed,' they wouldn't have to cry, would they?"

"I guess not," Alisa said. "Are babies a lot of trouble?" she wondered out loud.

Mother laughed as she put her glue gun down. "Babies do need care. But lots of people still want babies. Why do you think people like babies?" She sat down at the table and took a roll of ribbon, snipped off a piece, and began to make a fancy bow.

"Because babies are cute. And it's fun to take them on walks in their stroller," Alisa said. "I see Anne do that with her baby brother. And her baby brother laughs so hard when Anne plays peekaboo with him."

Mother said, "I'm glad I wanted a baby a long time ago. Now I have my seven-year-old Alisa to keep me company. What about you, Alisa? Will you be happy when we have a new baby in our family?"

"Yeah . . . but I kind of like being the only kid in this family." Alisa wasn't sure they needed any more kids. "I hope you'll still have time to play with me after we get a new baby," she said.

Mother pushed away the wreath she was working on and gave Alisa a big hug.

"I've told you many times how much I love you. You will always be my girl, Alisa. You don't ever have to be afraid that I won't have time for you. I like to do things with you. And you are getting so big now. You do so many things for yourself—like taking a bath and hanging up your clothes. Why, you're big enough to help Dad and me take care of our new baby."

Alisa still wasn't sure. She looked at her mother. "It's hard to believe a baby is growing in you right now. What do you think? Will the baby be a boy or a girl?"

"We don't know yet. But soon the doctor will do a test that will be able to tell us," Mother said. "But one thing we know now. It can kick."

"Is our baby kicking now?" Alisa asked.

"Yes, Alisa," Mother said. "Put your hand right here and you can feel the baby moving."

"Ooh, I can," Alisa said. "The baby is really moving."

"Isn't that exciting?" Mother said as she gave Alisa a little squeeze.

Alisa had lots to think about as Mother flipped the wreath over to fasten a hook on the back. "Will the baby have to sleep in my room? I don't think there would be room for another bed. I know how much baby stuff Anne's little brother has. My room could get crowded."

"Oh, no." Mother held up the finished wreath to admire. "The baby will have this room! All my crafts will be moved to the basement. Would you like to see the new curtains I bought for the baby's room?"

Mother held up the curtains for Alisa to see. "These curtains will be just right for a baby's room, don't you think? We'll put them up when Dad finishes painting the walls. He said you could pick out the color. What color do you think would look nice with these curtains?"

Alisa thought yellow would, because there were little yellow ducks all over the curtains. Mother thought that was a good choice too.

"I bet I know what the baby will sleep in—my baby crib!" Alisa was starting to get a little excited about getting ready for a new baby. "Can we get my crib down from the attic?"

"Not so fast!" Mother slowed her down. "It will be quite a while before the baby gets here. It will be about four months yet. Time enough to finish this room. We'll have to buy some new baby clothes too."

"Can I make something for the baby?" asked Alisa, "Maybe a picture or a toy?" While she was thinking about what she would make, Mother got out the vacuum to clean up the rug. When the vacuum finally stopped, Alisa asked another question. "Did the baby start growing a long time ago?"

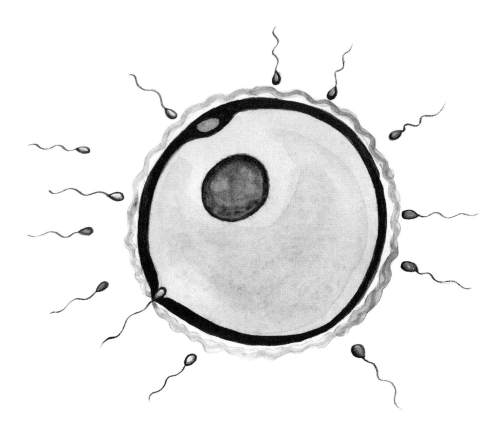

"Quite a while ago. It takes a baby nine months of growing before it is ready to be born. That's just as long as it took you to go through first grade."

"But what started the baby?" Alisa wanted to know.

"That's another miracle. God planned it so that it takes both a mother and a father. You see, every baby begins when two tiny parts join together and start to grow. One of these parts comes from the mother's body. It is called the *ovum*. The part that comes from the father's body is called the *sperm*."

"You mean daddies help babies start?" Alisa was getting another surprise.

"Of course," Mother pinched her cheek. "You are Daddy's girl too, aren't you?"

Alisa laughed, "That's what he says every time he swings me around and around. But how do daddies help babies start?"

"When a husband and wife love each other, they show it in many ways," Mother began.

"I know, they kiss each other and hug."

"That's right," said Mother. "They do things for each other, and they want to be together always."

"Is that why a bride and groom get married?"

"Yes, God is happy when two people decide to get married and start their life together with His blessing," Mother continued. "He made them for living together and showing their love to each other all their lives. At special times, they like to hold each other very close. God made their bodies so they fit together in a wonderful way.

"At those times, the sperm from the man's body can go into the woman's body. Sometimes a sperm and an ovum join in the mother's body. That is when a new baby begins."

"And that's why a baby belongs to both her father and her mother!" Now Alisa understood.

"Yes, that's the way God planned it! Both mother and father have a part in making the baby, but God has the biggest part. God blesses the mother and father and this new life as it grows and grows."

"Praise the LORD . . . He blesses your children within you." (Psalm 147:12–13)

Dad Is Home

"So this is where my family is!" Dad was home. "Have you two been hiding on me? Or should I say three?" he asked.

"Three?" Alisa wondered why Dad said that. Then she said, "Oh, I know what you mean. We've just been talking about the baby."

"Good! And what have you ordered? A boy or a girl?"

Alisa had to think about that. "We don't know that yet. But we will know for sure when we see it."

"Oh, really?" Dad laughed. "And how will you know then?"

"Because baby boys' bodies are like their daddies. And baby girls' bodies are like their mommies. Right?"

"That's right!" said Dad. "Both boys and girls have the body parts they need to become fathers or mothers when they grow up."

"But what are those parts?" Alisa wanted to know.

Mother answered, "When a baby girl is born, she already has the female parts she needs. A girl's uterus, you know, is inside her body. And she has a *vagina* that connects the uterus with the outside at an opening between the one for urine and the place for bowel movements."

"If girls have the female parts they need to become a mother someday, what parts do boys have so they can become fathers when they grow up?" asked Alisa.

"Well, on the boy's body," Dad said, "the male parts you can see are the penis and the scrotum. The part that looks a little like a finger is called the *penis*."

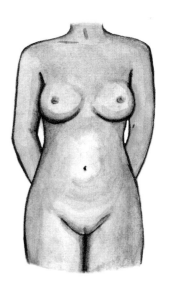

"That is where the urine comes out," Mother explained. "Also, when a boy becomes a man, at certain times sperm will pass out through the penis."

"The *scrotum* is the sac behind the penis," Dad continued. "The scrotum holds the *testicles*. After a boy grows up, the testicles start making the sperm I told you about."

"Boys and girls are really different," Alisa said. "I wonder which is the most important."

"There are many ways in which boys and girls are the same," Mother reminded her. "They both can grow, think, feel, and love. It is interesting that God planned for just about the same number of boys and girls to be born. So both of them must be important to Him."

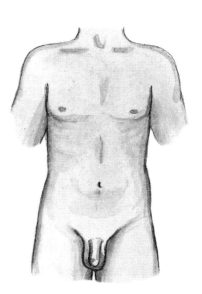

"It's not a matter of being more or less important. Boys and girls, men and women, are different. And we need each other. We help each other, and share and care for each other," said Dad. "This is God's plan for our lives. God's plans are always good, especially His plan to care for us through Jesus, who forgives us and saves us. God's plans are more than good; they are great!"

"See what kind of love the Father has given to us, that we should be called children of God." (1 John 3:1)

Loving and Caring for Each Other

"Alisa," Mother called, "will you please come and set the table for supper? It's almost time to eat."

"Coming!" Alisa followed the good smells into the kitchen. As she put the knives and forks beside the plates on the table, a big round pizza came steaming out of the oven. It smelled delicious! Mother poured the milk and told Alisa to call Dad to supper.

"I'm as hungry as a bear," he said as he sat down and put his napkin on his lap.

"Me too," Alisa echoed.

When everyone was sitting down, they folded their hands to pray: "Come, Lord Jesus, be our Guest. And let these gifts to us be blessed. Amen."

"Is the new baby one of God's gifts to us?" Alisa asked as soon as she had helped herself to a piece of pizza.

"The baby will be God's gift to all of us in this family," Dad agreed. "We will all enjoy the baby. We can all help take care of it too."

"Isn't it the mothers who take care of the babies?" Alisa asked.

As Dad cut another piece of pizza for her, he said, "Fathers and brothers and sisters can all help keep babies clean and comfortable and make them feel happy and loved."

"Did you help take care of me when I was a baby?" Alisa asked her dad as she took a big drink of milk.

"Did I ever!" Dad remembered. "When you were little, you had tummyaches almost every night after supper. I used to put you on your tummy and lay you on my lap. I'd bounce you a little, then pat you a lot. That seemed to be the only thing that would make you stop crying."

Alisa wanted to help take care of the baby too. "Will I be able to hold the baby on my lap?"

"Sure, you'll be able to hold the baby," Dad promised, "as long as it doesn't wiggle too much."

"Will I be able to feed it too?" Alisa wondered.

"No, not at first," replied Mother. "Newborn babies need only milk, and I plan to nurse the new baby just as I did you."

"You mean you're going to be the nurse if the baby gets sick?"

"No, no!" laughed Mother, "I should have explained that word *nurse*. When babies are born, their mothers have milk in their breasts to feed them. This is how God provides just the kind of food the baby needs. The baby snuggles close to Mother's breast and drinks the milk and feels very much loved."

"Babies don't know very many things when they are born," said Dad. "But no one has to teach them how to suck. They know that! They suck on fingers and pacifiers. They suck almost anything they can get into their mouths."

Alisa laughed at that; then she remembered, "Anne's little brother drinks from a bottle with a nipple on it. I wonder why he gets his milk that way."

Mother knew about that too. "Some mothers feed their babies milk from bottles. That milk helps them grow strong and healthy too. Those mothers also love their babies very much. They hold them close, cuddle them, talk to them, and smile at them."

"You and I will be able to help feed the baby later, Alisa," Dad said, "when it is ready for cereal and fruit juice and baby food."

"And we can talk to it and play with it and love it!" said Alisa.

"We sure can," Dad said as he picked her up. "And that's a very important part. That's what families are for—loving each other. It's all part of God's plan."

Alisa smiled and said, "What a special blessing it will be when this baby is born into our family and is born into God's family too!"

Jesus said, "Let the little children come to Me . . .
for to such belongs the kingdom of heaven." (Matthew 19:14)